PRESSING PLANTS

PRESSING PLANTS

Janet Lynch-Watson

FREDERICK MULLER LTD.

First published in Great Britain, 1975
by Frederick Muller Limited, London, NW2 6LE

Copyright © 1975 Janet Lynch-Watson

ISBN 0 584 62050 0

Printed in Great Britain by The Optima Press
Leicester and bound by Cox and Wyman, Fakenham

Have you ever thought that you would like to see a primrose blossoming at the same time as a rose, or a snowdrop side by side with a poppy?

If you press flowers you are able to do just this. Pressing plants removes the moisture from the flowers and leaves. It also flattens them. They will keep in this condition for many years. Some will keep their colour better than others. However, those that fade or change their colour often turn out to be the most attractive.

Once you have pressed your flowers, leaves, stalks or whatever part of the plant you have chosen, there are many ways you can use your pressings. You will be able to use them to decorate greetings cards, stationery, finger plates, pictures, mobiles, lampshades and many other things.

Flower pressing was a popular Victoria hobby, particularly among young ladies. For many years after the Victorian period it was almost forgotten as a craft, but recently interest in it has been revived.

EQUIPMENT

The only essential pieces of equipment are some absorbent paper and some means of applying enough pressure to flatten the plants. Any heavy weight will do.

The best paper to use is blotting paper, preferably white. However, blotting paper is expensive and very good results can be obtained with newspaper, especially if you choose the more expensive newsprint that has been less heavily inked.

You can press the flowers or leaves in a large book with a heavy pile of books or bricks on top. Or you can make yourself a simple press.

MAKING FLOWER PRESSES

Cut out two pieces of hardboard or plywood to a convenient size, perhaps twenty centimetres square. Your flowers can then be pressed between these boards. The best way to do this is to put the flowers between sheets of blotting paper and put the blotting paper between sheets of folded newspaper. If desired, several layers can be pressed at once between the boards. One way to exert pressure on the boards is to use clamps.

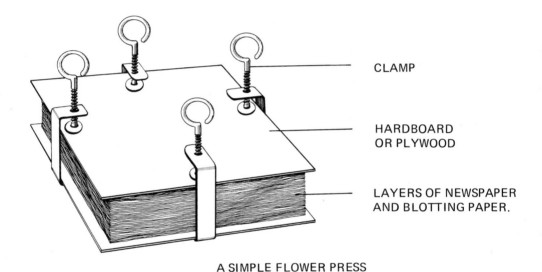

CLAMP

HARDBOARD
OR PLYWOOD

LAYERS OF NEWSPAPER
AND BLOTTING PAPER.

A SIMPLE FLOWER PRESS

These should be screwed down firmly. It does not matter if you unscrew the clamps at a later date in order to insert more flowers but care should be taken not to disturb those in the process of being pressed.

The sort of tennis racquet press that has a nut, bolt and spring, in each could be easily converted into a plant press.

Another method would be to use very strong elastic bands to press the boards together — instead of clamps.

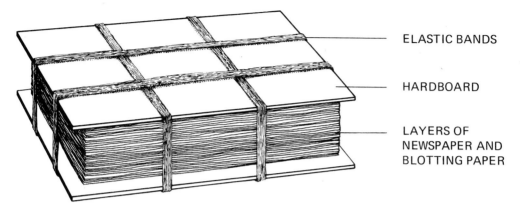

ELASTIC BANDS

HARDBOARD

LAYERS OF
NEWSPAPER AND
BLOTTING PAPER

FLOWER PRESS USING STRONG ELASTIC BANDS

A smaller press, about 10 x 15 centimetres, made in the same way and using elastic bands, is very useful as a pocket press to take on walks and outings. Many plants wilt quickly after picking and need to be pressed as soon as possible.

PRESSING

Do not think that only people who live in the country or have large gardens can take up flower pressing. One of the joys of this hobby is that weeds and the most humble flowers often make wonderful pressed flowers. Nor do you even have to use flowers. Leaves and grasses can be just as attractive when pressed.

Here are some hints about choosing plants and pressing them.

Only pick dry flowers and leaves. This means not only that it is inadvisable to pick flowers when there has been rain, but also that you should not gather flowers early in the morning when they are still damp from the dew. If they are at all wet when pressed they will turn mouldy.

Remember that the flatter the shape of a plant is, the better it will press, so avoid bulky plants. A rose, for instance, is far too thick. However, it is possible to press individual rose petals. They acquire a beautiful soft, silky texture when pressed.

Some flowers, like the daisy, have a thick centre, but these can be pressed successfully. When you place them on the blotting paper gently flatten the centre with your finger.

Some flowers like the primrose have a small tube behind the petals. Cut this off with a sharp pair of scissors very close to the petals. This makes the flower absolutely flat for pressing. However, be careful that this treatment does not cause the whole flower to disintegrate. It can only be done with some flowers.

It is quite possible to press a flower that is not flat, providing it is not *too* thick. The best method is to place the flower on the paper face down and to place the second piece of blotting paper very carefully over it. Try to press down any parts of the flower or stem that stick out at the back and, at the same time keep the face of the flower flat.

The pansy is a flower that needs to be treated in this way, as it is necessary to press part of the stalk.

Other hints on the pressing and preparation of flowers and leaves are given

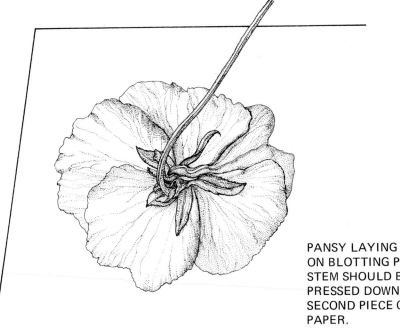

PANSY LAYING FLAT
ON BLOTTING PAPER.
STEM SHOULD BE GENTLY
PRESSED DOWN WITH A
SECOND PIECE OF BLOTTING
PAPER.

in the next section of this book which deals with individual plants and their treatment.

When you have arranged your flowers for pressing, it is important to label them. The easiest way to do this is to put a slip of paper with the flowers in the press or book. If this sticks out a little it will be easy to see. It should have the name of the flower or leaf and the date that pressing began. It is most important to note the date so that you know when your pressed flowers will be ready.

Most flowers and leaves take at least three weeks to press. If they are thick flowers, it may be necessary to change the blotting paper after the first week because the moisture contained in the plant will have dampened the blotting paper. It is best to leave the plants for six to eight weeks to be sure they are properly pressed.

You may need to store your pressed plants in order to use the press again. Make sure they are fully dried and flattened and then store them between sheets of paper. Tissue paper or lining paper will do very well. The pages of a large book can also be used for this purpose. Again it is a good idea to label the pages so that you can find the plants easily.

Don't throw away the blotting paper you have used for pressing. Unless it is very badly stained you can use it again.

FLOWERS

Here is a list of flowers that you may come across and some notes on how to press them.

ALYSSUM This is a garden plant. The flower head has a mass of little white flowers. Press the whole head. There is also a most attractive yellow alyssum which presses well.

AUBRETIA This rockery plant does not keep its colour well; it fades to a mottled purple. However, it can be striking when arranged in a design.

BIRD'S FOOT TREFOIL Yellow flowers are generally best for retaining their colour and Bird's Foot Trefoil or Grandmother's Toenails as it is sometimes called is no exception. It is a common plant frequently found on grassland.

BLUEBELL The blue of this flower faces rapidly and thus this is a disappointing one to press. However, you may decide to do a few for their pretty shape.

BROOM This is a shrub which comes in many colours, the most usual being yellow. The individual flowers press very well.

BUTTERCUP Another good yellow flower to press. There are many ways to press buttercups.

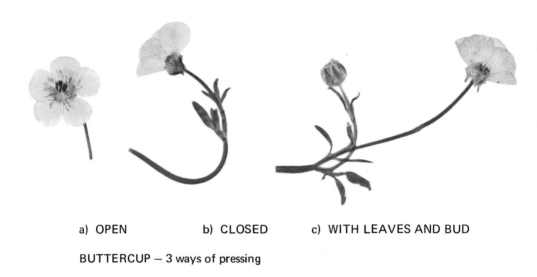

a) OPEN   b) CLOSED   c) WITH LEAVES AND BUD

BUTTERCUP — 3 ways of pressing

CANTERBURY BELL The flowers of this garden plant are a lovely clear blue and an attractive bell shape.

CHRYSANTHEMUM The flowers of this autumn plant are obviously too fat to press but individual petals of some varieties can be pressed if they are flat enough.

CLEMATIS This is a shrub generally seen growing up the walls of houses. The most common varieties have mauve or purple flowers. Press the petals separately. They usually turn brown. The stalks are also useful.

CLOVER A common enough plant and a good one to press. The petals can be spread out from the centre or pressed all in one direction as in the illustration.

COW PARSLEY You are not likely to have much difficulty in finding this common weed. Press a small head or part of a head.

CYCLAMEN The small, outdoor varieties are the ones to press. Like Bluebells their colour fades. However, the shape can be attractive.

DAISY These are easy enough to find. Press the centre down with your finger and nip off the stalk before covering with the second piece of blotting paper. When pressed the back is as attractive as the front.

DAHLIA Like chrysanthemums, individual petals are worth pressing providing they are flat enough.

DELPHINIUM This is a blue garden flower that retains its colour very well. As it is a somewhat bulky flower, it is easier to press if you dismantle the petals first.

DAY LILY This is a garden flower with pale green spear-like leaves and orange flowers. These press well.

FORGET-ME-NOT In some parts this flower grows like a weed and won't be hard to find. The smaller heads can be pressed whole. The individual flowers look very attractive when pressed, but being small they take time to do.

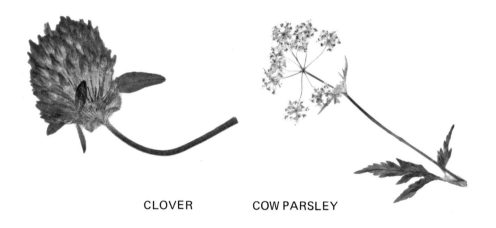

CLOVER   COW PARSLEY

FORSYTHIA   This is a shrub that blossoms early in the year with yellow flowers. These appear before the leaves. It is a good chance to start pressing at the beginning of spring.

FUCHSIA   These need long and heavy pressing as the seed head is very hard. The deep pink flowers turn almost black but are well worth pressing for the shape of the flower alone.

GOLDEN ROD   These very tall garden flowers appear in the late summer. They can be pressed if you use just the top few centimetres of the plant. The curve at the top of the plant is a useful shape for composition.

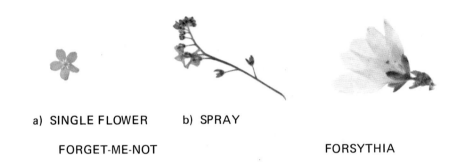

a) SINGLE FLOWER   b) SPRAY

FORGET-ME-NOT   FORSYTHIA

GROUND IVY   This is a weed commonly seen on waste ground. It usually grows ten to thirty centimetres high and has small purple flowers growing from the base of the leaves which are found all the way up the stem. The top few centimetres of this plant are very attractive when pressed.

HAWKWEED   This is another common weed that has several dandelion-like flowers on a stem. It can be pressed when flowering. It is also attractive if it is pressed when the white fluffy seed heads appear.

HONEYSUCKLE   This shrub is found growing up walls, trees or in hedges. The flower heads are best taken to pieces for pressing. You can always assemble them again when using them. They turn a deep brown.

HONEYSUCKLE   HYDRANGEA

HYDRANGEA   The individual flowers can be pressed. Some tend to be leathery but they turn interesting almost metallic colours.

LABURNAM   This is a tree usually found in gardens with long yellow drooping stems of flowers. You can press a whole stem or the individual flowers. These turn cream. Don't forget that the black seeds of the laburnam found after flowering are very poisonous.

LADY'S BEDSTRAW   Another very common weed that has a small yellow flower. Press a stem with leaves for a delicate lacey effect. It dries to a dark colour.

LARKSPUR   This garden plant is very like a delphinium but shorter. The flowers of larkspur, like those of the delphinium, should be dismantled.

LOOSESTRIFE   This garden plant has leaves growing all the way up the stems. Yellow flowers grow from the bases of the leaves. The flowers press well.

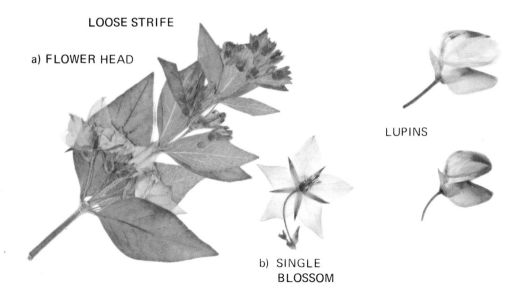

LOOSE STRIFE

a) FLOWER HEAD

LUPINS

b) SINGLE BLOSSOM

LUPIN These take time to press as each individual flower must be taken off the stem and pressed separately. There are many colours that turn attractive shades when pressed.

MARIGOLD The heads of marigolds are too thick to press, but if you have a good deal of patience you may care to press some petals. They turn a beautiful transparent gold.

NIPPLEWORT This is another 'dandelion-like' weed similar to hawkweed but with smaller flower heads. It can be best pressed when it is in bud or after the seeds have appeared. Remove the fluffy seeds first. The pattern of the stems has a pleasant branching effect.

PANSY Garden pansies press well. The colours fade gradually to quite interesting colours. The smaller wild pansy is just as good as the garden sort. Press the back of the flower with a piece of stem as well as the petals, otherwise the flower will disintegrate.

PHLOX This is a garden plant. It has a long leafy stalk topped by a head of several flowers. These can be white, pink, red or mauve. The white ones become almost transparent when pressed, but they are very attractive if they are used in a design on a coloured background. Cut off the little tube at the back of each flower.

PINKS These are flowers in the carnation family. The petals have to be pressed separately, which is a pity. The band of colour that is found on some varieties makes a pleasing effect when they are pressed.

POLYANTHUS These are excellent for pressing. Cut off the tube at the back. The best for keeping their colour are the yellow varieties. The orange ones go pinky grey and reds and purples turn almost black.

POPPY Poppies are hard to press but worth the effort. Gently cut away most of the seed head in the centre and arrange the petals face down and flat. Separate petals are also useful. The yellow poppy becomes creamy orange and the red turns purple.

PRIMROSE and PRIMULA Like the polyanthus these are excellent pressers. Remove the tube at the back.

PULMONARIA This is a garden plant that appears in early spring with pink or blue flowers and a speckled hairy leaf. The flowers do not always retain their colour but they are a good shape.

PURPLE
PRIMULA

PRIMROSE

POPPY   Yellow poppy has
turned orange

ROSE As has already been said, only the petals can be pressed, not the whole flower. The flatter the petals are the better they will press. They do not keep their colours but turn various shades of cream and brown.

SAXIFRAGE This is a popular rockery plant that looks like a bright green cushion. There are several varieties. They mostly press well but sometimes their hard centres need to be flattened by pressing on them first.

SCARLET PIMPERNEL Like forget-me-nots, scarlet pimpernels take time to prepare for pressing because they are so small. They are useful for small pictures.

SUNFLOWER The small varieties that have yellow petals of about four centimetres long are the ones to press. Press each petal separately. You will find that the veins of the petal which are normally invisible, turn brown.

TULIP In many ways tulips are unsatisfactory for pressing. However, it is worth doing a few of the very pretty petals. There are some most interesting colours and these can be used for cutting out mock flowers or berries for a particular picture.

VIOLETS Although their colour soon fades, the shape makes the worth pressing.

ASPARAGUS FERN   BEECH and COPPER BEECH LEAVES

WALLFLOWER   It is best to press separate petals, which have beautiful colours.

WINTER JASMINE   There are not many flowers that you can press in December, but this yellow shrub is one. Cut off the tube at the back.

These are only a selection of flowers suitable for pressing. You will find many more.

LEAVES

Leaves vary in shape, colour, the pattern of the veins, thickness and in many other ways. This means they are very suitable to be pressed as there is such a range to choose from.

Thick leaves will not press well, so avoid these unless they can be picked in the spring when they are still tender.

ASPARAGUS   We usually think of asparagus as something to eat, but the ferny fronds of the asparagus plant turn brown when pressed and are very pretty.

BEECH   Like most tree leaves, the time to gather beech leaves is in the early spring when they have that transparent look before they become coarse. There are also the copper beech leaves which has very striking leaves.

BIRCH   Again these leaves are best pressed in early spring. They are also attractive in the autumn when they change colour.

BLACKBERRY   These are good both in spring and in autumn. In spring the leaves have a greeny-grey underside which is pleasant. In autumn the leaves turn red.

BRYONY   This is useful for the triangular-shaped leaves. The curly tendrils can also be pressed.

CHERRY   There are many sorts of cherry trees. The red-leaved variety can be pressed in spring, and the green-leaved ones can sometimes be pressed when turning yellow and pink if they are not too thick.

CINERARIA   These are the grey, spiky-leaved plants often seen in formal gardens and parks. They press very well.

CINERARIA LEAF   GERANIUM LEAVES

GERANIUM   This is the sort of geranium people grow in pots and which should really be called pelargonium, for a real geranium is something quite different. However its heart-shaped leaves press to an unusual brown-beige colour.

HERB ROBERT   This common wayside weed can be used for its flowers, but even better are its leaves which have a delicate lacy pattern.

LIME LEAF   MAPLE LEAVES

HOLLY   These leaves are very coarse but if you press them when they are very young, they can be successfully used. Nearly all varieties turn almost black. They are useful in designing Christmas cards.

HORSE CHESTNUT   These must be picked very young. The pattern of six leaves makes an unusual shape when pressed.

IVY   These do not press very well for they tend to be leathery. However, they can be used with holly in Christmas designs.

LABURNAM   The new leaves of the laburnam are very green, and the colour remains after pressing. As well as single leaves, several on one stem make a useful arrangement.

LIME   The early lime leaves are almost transparent. At that stage they are suitable for pressing.

MAPLE   There are many types of maple from pale green to the red of the ornamental varieties. The early leaves are soft enough to press and their shape most attractive.

MAYWEED   This is a weed best known for its pale yet bright green leaves and rather unpleasant smell. The leaves press to a beautiful golden-green colour.

OAK The leaves need to be young. They are worth pressing for their shape rather than their colour.

POINSETTIA   This is an indoor pot plant that is seen at Christmastime. It has scarlet leaves which turn purple-red when pressed.

PRIVET This dull hedge has useful leaves. The early ones press to a pleasant green and are useful for their small size.

RASPBERRY   These leaves are a good shape and have very attractive grey undersides.

ROSE The new red leaves of a rose are amongst the finest to press. The underside becomes a beautiful grey-pink. Pick about five on a stem as well as individual leaves.

ROWAN   If picked when young, one stem makes a useful spray of leaves when pressed.

SENECIO   This is a shrub often used to make small hedges. It has small yellow flowers in the summer and strange leaves that look as though they are covered with cotton wool on one side.

SUMACH   These are only worth picking when they turn red. The colour is very striking and the smaller leaves are thin enough to press.

SYCAMORE This must be pressed in spring before it becomes too coarse.

SENECIO LEAVES   SUMACH LEAVES

TOADFLAX The 'Ivy-leaved' variety is very good to press. The curving stems with small leaves and flowers spaced along them have a most attractive shape. Press whole stems.

VETCH This is another interesting plant on account of its shape. Press stems and tendrils.

WHITEBEAM This is a tree that has 'cotton-wool' leaves rather like senecio. Press them when they are young.

YARROW The leaves of this wild plant are worth pressing for their ferny shape.

YEW The new pale green leaves of yew can be pressed very effectively.

STALKS. GRASS, FERNS, FRUITS, etc.

Stalks, grass, ferns and fruits can be used, as well as leaves and flowers. You will get into the habit of keeping your eyes open for anything useful.

STALKS Look out for suitable stalks. It is useful to have a variety of lengths and shapes. Primula, primrose, polyanthus, clover, buttercup all have pleasantly curved delicate stalks which are very useful.

GRASS Don't despise grass. Some of the wild grasses have beautiful lacey formations. There are many different varieties to choose and, unless the seeds are too bulky, most of them are suitable for pressing.

POLYANTHUS STEM   PRIMULA STEM

DIFFERENT PRESSED GRASSES

FERNS There are many varieties of ferns. Many are good for pressing.

GOOSEGRASS This needs a special mention. This is the plant that sticks to people's clothes. The arrangement of the leaves and the little round green balls or fruits make it very effective when pressed. Press it gently to avoid spoiling the shape of the fruits.

HONESTY PODS They can be used in two ways. When the pods first appear they are small and green and make an interesting shape when pressed. When the pods are fully developed remove the two outer layers and the seeds. This reveals the delicate silver membrane in the middle. It is not necessary to press this unless it is to flatten the stalk, as the pod is already dried.

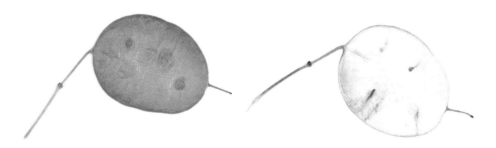

HONESTY PODS AT DIFFERENT STAGES OF DEVELOPMENT

POPPY BUDS If these are picked at an early enough stage they are not too fat to press. The way in which the stalk usually curves with the weight of the bud makes a pleasing shape.

OLD MAN'S BEARD The feathery fruits are interesting to press. You may find it easier to do if you take them to pieces first.

THINGS TO MAKE AND DO WITH PRESSED FLOWERS

Now that you have pressed some flowers and leaves you may be wondering what you are going to do with them when they are ready to be taken from the press. Here are some ideas on what they can be used for.

FLOWER PICTURES

The most obvious thing is to arrange them into a picture. In this way you are able to create pictures that you would need great skill to paint.

Here are some points about designing a flower picture.

A paintbrush is helpful for moving the pressed flowers around until you have them arranged exactly as you like.

Take care not to overcrowd your work with too many flowers and leaves. The spaces between the leaves and flowers are just as important a part of the design as the leaves and flowers themselves. Overcrowded designs generally look fussy and do not show off the shape and colour of the plants to their best advantage.

Don't be afraid to experiment with your flower designs. You can construct your own varieties of plants. Primroses growing with horse chestnut leaves look very striking! You are able to mix the flowers of different seasons. Try spring flowers in a design with autumn leaves.

When you have got your design as you want it, there are two ways in which you can stick it to your mounting card.

1. GLUE. Use only a very little glue - just enough to make a petal or leaf stick to the background. When your picture is finished you can frame it and cover it with glass. This is necessary protection for the flowers if you wish to keep the picture for any length of time.

2. An alternative method is to use transparent plastic sheeting. This has the advantage that it is much cheaper than framing. It gives good protection and your work can still be framed even if you have used the sheeting first.

As the sheeting is adhesive on one side the easiest method of using it is to put the flowers straight into position on to the adhesive side.

Arranging your design and then trying to cover it with the transparent plastic sheeting is not very satisfactory as the sheeting attracts the flowers, making them move out of position.

A PRESSED FLOWER PICTURE USING ROSE LEAVES, WILD GRASS AND SAXIFRAGE FLOWERS

Cut the sheeting to the correct size. It is best to allow a margin on your background, so cut the sheeting smaller than the card. As well as making it easier to manage, this margin gives your work a professional look.

Peel the backing off the transparent plastic sheeting and lay the sheeting, sticky side up, on a piece of paper. With your arranged design at your side transfer the flowers and leaves one by one on to the sheeting. Smooth them into place with a paintbrush. Remember that those flowers that are in front of the design need to be put on first, and that those that should be on the left side of the design need to be put on the right and vice versa. Then lay the sheeting on to your card sticky side down and smooth into place. You will soon get quite good at doing this and may eventually be able to design a picture straight on to the plastic sheeting and know what it will look like when viewed from the other side.

These pictures make ideal gifts and can be sent quite cheaply and conveniently by post.

GREETINGS CARDS

Using a pressed flower design to make greetings cards gives you the chance to use several small arrangements. You can adapt your material to the individual tastes of the person receiving the card. For instance, if your mother is very fond of the poppies that appear each summer in your garden, she will be delighted to receive a card made of the same poppies at a time like Christmas when there won't be a poppy to be seen.

Try doing some designs on coloured card as they can be most effective.

GIFT TAGS, STATIONERY ETC.

Gift tags can be made with one or two flowers under a piece of trans-

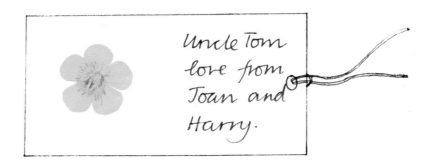

GIFT TAG DECORATED WITH PRESSED FLOWERS

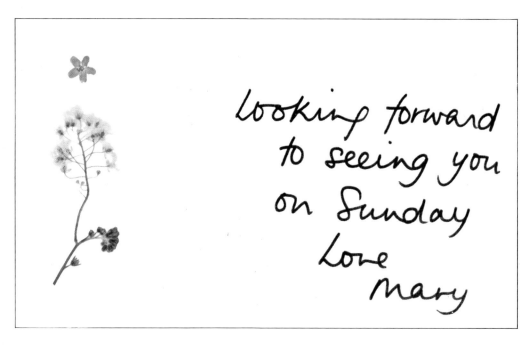

Looking forward to seeing you on Sunday Love Mary

POSTCARD DECORATED WITH PRESSED FLOWERS

parent plastic sheeting about two centimetres square and stuck on to a small, rectangular piece of card. Leave a space to write the greeting and attach some coloured ribbon.

Quite ordinary writing paper can be transformed into something very special just by putting a flower or leaf in the left hand corner and covering it with transparent sheeting.

The same can be done with plain post cards, either for your own use or as a present for someone else.

Book marks, note pads and other stationery items can be decorated in a similar fashion.

A BOOK OF FLOWERS

As a present for someone who is fond of flowers, a book of pressed flower pictures would give great pleasure. There are various themes that you could use in such a book - the seasons, a person's favourite flowers, the flowers from a particular garden or place or a selection based on the language of flowers. Flowers have traditional meanings and you could probably get a book from your local library to help you.

Another idea would be to make a nature book. There could hardly be a better way of illustrating what a flower or leaf look like than to have the actual flower. You could also show the various stages of bud, flower and fruit.

FINGER PLATES

Finger plates are the panels on doors that protect the door from finger marks. It is possible to buy very expensive wood or china ones that have painted flowers on them. However, you can go one better and make some with real flowers. Plain transparent perspex finger plates are sold at iron-mongers shops and do not cost very much. Cut out a thick paper or card-board backing the same size as the finger plate. Arrange your flower de-sign on this and either glue it on to the card or cover it with transparent plastic sheeting.

A design with some long curving stalks will be useful and most suitable in this case. Place it under the finger plate when it is being screwed to the door.

It is a good idea to mark where the screw holes will come by gently piercing the card. Avoid putting flowers or leaves over them.

FINGER PLATE WITH
PRESSED FLOWER DESIGN

A WINDOW PICTURE

This is a 'see-through' picture that you can look at from both sides and which, if hung in a window, looks particularly attractive with the light shining through it. If you use some of the more transparent flowers and leaves as part of the design you will get the best effect from the light.

You need to have a stiff frame so cut out two pieces of card to make a frame of double thickness. Next cut out two pieces of transparent plastic sheeting, a little larger than the 'hole' of the frame. Peel the backing off one piece and lay it down sticky side up.

Arrange your pattern on the sticky side remembering to choose flowers and leaves that will look all right on both sides. When the design is finished lay the other piece of sheeting over the top (both sticky sides together with the flowers etc. in between). Lay this between the two sides of the cardboard frame which should now be glued together.

LINE FOR FOLDING
CARD BOARD

TWO LAYERS OF
PLASTIC SHEETING
WITH PRESSED FLOWERS
SANDWICHED BETWEEN
THEM

CARDBOARD FRAME
BEFORE FOLDING
AND GLUEING

WINDOW PICTURE

A mobile for a child's room could be made by making several small window pictures and hanging them from a piece of wire.

A FRIEZE FOR A CHILD'S ROOM

A frieze with a pressed flower design is most effective if the wall you intend to stick it on is very plain. You can then arrange your flowers on a long strip of transparent plastic sheeting and stick this straight on to the wall.

If the wall has a pattern on it, you will have to stick the sheeting on to some plain paper or card before putting it on the wall.

LAMPSHADES

Pressed flowers and leaves show up well on lampshades with the light shining through them.

To cover a whole shade with transparent plastic sheeting can be awkward unless the shade is the shape of a plain tube. If it has sloping sides it is easier to cut out small pieces of plastic sheeting — round or oval shapes look good — and stick these panels to a plain lampshade when you have arranged some flowers on them.

Another method is to stick the flowers straight on to the lampshade with glue and protect them with a coat of lacquer.

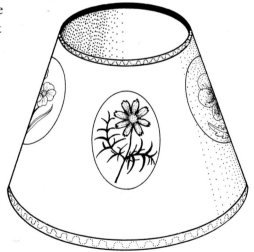

LAMPSHADE DECORATED
WITH PRESSED FLOWERS

A WASTE PAPER BASKET

Large plastic containers such as the one gallon ice-cream boxes are a suitable size for waste paper baskets. These too can be decorated with pressed flowers arranged under panels of transparent sheeting.

JEWELLERY

There are several ways in which you can use your pressed flowers to make simple and attractive jewellery. Here are two suggestions.

Stationers stock packs of round plain cardboard badges with a fastening pin on the back. Pressed flowers can be used to decorate these. Cover your arrangement with a piece of plastic sheeting cut a little larger than the badge. Make a series of small cuts all round the overlap. This will enable you to fold under the overlap at the back of the badge more neatly.

A pendant is not difficult to make. Cut a piece of thick white cardboard to a suitable shape — square, diamond, circle etc. This will form the base. Pierce the top to make a small hole. Natural wood, sand-papered and varnished, is another attractive base providing the wood is not too thick. The wood which surrounds honey combs is ideal for sawing into oblong pendants. Metal or plastic cut to a suitable shape can also be used. Decorate the pendant with pressed flowers, using one of the methods already described. To thread the pendant on to a leather thong or a chain, it is necessary to fix a 'jump' ring through the hole in the pendant. You can purchase these very cheaply from hobby shops or jewellers. You could use a piece of thick fuse wire.

A SMALL FLOWER POT

Many shops sell mousses and desserts in transparent containers that do not have any writing on them. A small but useful flower vase can be made by decorating them with pressed flowers. The method is described in the sections for lampshades and waste paper baskets.

This method, using small pieces of transparent plastic sheeting over a flower design can be used for decorating many articles around the house —

writing cases, comb cases, mats, biscuit tins, children's furniture, coat hangers, pencil boxes and many more.

You will have probably plenty of ideas of your own for using your pressed flowers.